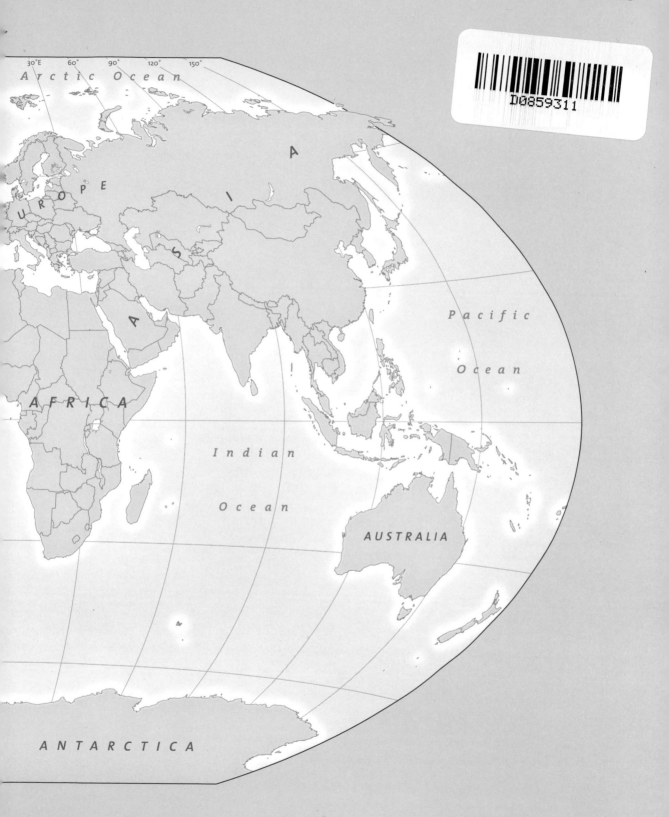

Colombia

Anita Croy

Ulrich Oslender and Mauricio Pardo, Consultants

Contents

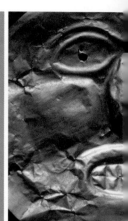

Foreword

Colombia has the second-largest Spanish-speaking population in the world and is the fifth-largest Latin American country. A variety of landscapes host a range of regional cultures and more than sixty Indian groups. Rain forests, savannahs, mountains, and 1,800 miles (2,900 km) of coastline on two oceans make Colombia the world's second-most biodiverse country.

Conflict has been constant in Colombia's history. Spanish conquerors made unions with Indian women, but almost killed out native cultures. Only small groups survived, mainly in remote locations. Many enslaved Africans and their descendants intermarried with whites and Indians. A population of mixed descent and distinct regional cultures developed.

After wars against Spain brought independence in the 19th century, conservative and liberal parties fought many civil wars. Despite the turmoil, Colombia was home to a prominent elite of intellectuals and poets. Bogotá came to be called "the South American Athens."

In the first half of the 20th century, exports of coffee, bananas, and oil boomed. Industries developed in several growing cities. The peace ended in 1948, when violence between political opponents in rural areas caused some 300,000 deaths.

The violence fell by 1964, but after the 1970s poverty and the drug trade again fueled conflict. More than 100,000 civilians were killed by paramilitaries, guerrillas, the military, and criminals; three million people became refugees. Today, land-ownership and wealth are concentrated in the hands of a few people, while half the population lives in poverty. Public education and health care are deficient, drug trafficking and corruption are common, and damage to the environment is at alarming levels.

Despite this, parts of the economy and culture have flourished, mainly in the larger cities. Exports have diversified. Roads, electricity supply, and communications have greatly improved. Colombian popular culture, fine arts, cuisine, and sports have fans around the world. Within Colombia, ethnic and African Colombian communities, despite being among the main victims of violence, take more part in public life.

Many Colombians believe that social equity and conflict resolution, and fighting corruption and drug trafficking, is necessary to enable the country to harness its cultural, social, economic, and environmental resources. If this can happen, Colombia will come closer to the peaceful and marvelous country its inhabitants have long deserved.

▲ **The official motto of Bogotá, Colombia's capital, reflects the city's height above sea level: "Bogotá, 2,600 meters closer to the stars."**

Mauricio Pardo
Universidad del Rosario

From the Snow to the Surf

FROM COLOMBIA'S HIGHEST mountain, Pico Cristóbal Colón, to the beaches near the historic city of Cartagena is a distance of only 120 miles (200 km). In that short trip—the same as traveling from Washington, D.C., to Philadelphia—the landscape is transformed from rugged, snow-capped mountains to a tropical, jungle-clad coast.

As well as mountains and rain forests, Colombia has some of the rainiest and driest spots on Earth, huge wetlands, rolling grasslands, and violent volcanoes. All this variety fits into one of the largest countries in South America. But Colombia is less important for its size than for its location. It controls the southern end of the narrow strip of land that joins the continent to Central and North America. For that reason, Colombia is often called "the gateway to South America."

◄ **A young man takes his horse for a swim on Colombia's Caribbean coast.**

WHAT'S THE WEATHER LIKE?

Although Colombia has distinct regions, its weather does not vary that much throughout the year. That is because the country lies near the Equator, halfway between the North and South Poles. As a result there are only two seasons: one dry period and one when it rains regularly.

The lowland areas are known as "hot country." The average temperature is a pleasant 75° F (24° C). In "cold country," which lies in the hills that cross the country, temperatures average only 55° F (13° C). The map opposite shows the physical features of Colombia. Labels on this map and on similar maps in this book identify most of the places pictured in each chapter.

Fast Facts

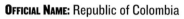

OFFICIAL NAME: Republic of Colombia
TYPE OF GOVERNMENT: Republic
CAPITAL: Bogotá
POPULATION: 44,379,598
OFFICIAL LANGUAGE: Spanish
MONETARY UNIT: Peso
AREA: 439,619 square miles (1,138,910 square kilometers)
BORDERING NATIONS: Brazil, Ecuador, Panama, Peru, and Venezuela
HIGHEST POINT: Pico Cristóbal Colón 5,775 meters (Pico Simón Bolívar is nearby and the same height)
LOWEST POINT: Pacific Ocean, sea level
MAJOR MOUNTAIN RANGES: Andes, Sierra Nevada de Santa Marta
MAJOR RIVERS: Magdalena, Cauca, Atrato, Sinú

Average Temperature & Rainfall

Average High/Low Temperatures; Yearly Rainfall
BOGOTÁ (MOUNTAINS):
   60° F (15° C) / 44° F (7° C); 31 in (80 cm)
CARTAGENA (COAST):
   88° F (31° C) / 76° F (24° C); 39 in (101 cm)
LETICIA (RAIN FOREST):
   86° F (30° C) / 71° F (22° C); 128 in (330 cm)
VILLAVICENCIO (PLAINS):
   95° F (35° C) / 70° F (21° C); 172 in (440 cm)

Caribbean Sea

Pacific Ocean

MAP KEY
Dry
☐ Semiarid
Tropical
■ Tropical wet
☐ Tropical dry
Highland
☐ Highland

0   mi   200
0   km   200

Isla del Providencia
Isla de San Andrés

Caribbean Sea

NICARAGUA

COSTA RICA

PANAMA

COLOMBIA

0   mi   200
0   km   200

COLOMBIA

Atlantic Ocean

Pacific Ocean

South America

Caribbean Sea

HELICOPTER OVER JUNGLE, page 11

SALT MINERS, page 15

Guajira Peninsula

Santa Marta

Barranquilla

FOOD VENDOR AND FORTRESS, page 11

Cartagena

BOY AND HORSE, pages 2, 6-7

Pico Cristóbal Colón (Highest point in Colombia) 18,947 ft 5,775 m

Valledupar

Sierra Nevada de Sta. Marta

Magdalena

Sincelejo

Simú

Cauca

PANAMA

Gulf of Urabá

Darien Gap

Turbo

GIRLS WITH UMBRELLA, page 12

Cúcuta

VENEZUELA

Chocó

Atrato

Baudó Mountains

DARIEN GAP, page 13

Quibdó

Medellín

Bucaramanga

Magdalena

COWBOYS, page 14

L l a n o s

Meta

Orinoco

Pacific Ocean

Cordillera Occidental

Cordillera Central

BURIED TOWN, page 10

Cordillera Oriental

Manizales

Armero

Bogotá

CITY SCENE, page 5

Meta

Vichada

Buenaventura

Ibagué

C O L O M B I A

Guaviare

Cauca

Cali

Neiva

Cordillera Occidental

Cordillera Central

Cordillera Oriental

Tierradentro Valley

Vaupés

Pasto

Caquetá

Apaporis

VOLCANO CRATER, page 12

MOUNTAIN VALLEY, page 14

EQUATOR

BRAZIL

Putumayo

Caquetá

ECUADOR

A M A Z O N

PERU

B A S I N

Amazon

MAP KEY

⊛   National capital

●   Selected city

+   Elevation

—   Pan-American Highway

0   miles   200

Physical Map

Coast to Coast

Colombia is unique in South America. It is the only country with coasts on two oceans, the Caribbean (an arm of the Atlantic) and the Pacific. The Caribbean coast forms Colombia's northern border, while the Pacific runs down its western side. Colombia has land borders from west to east with Ecuador, Peru, Brazil, and Venezuela. Finally, there is a short border with Panama in the north, on the isthmus, or neck of land, that leads to Central and North America.

About 20 percent of Colombia's population live on the Caribbean coast. As well as having some great

DEADLY RAIN

On the night of November 13, 1985, while the quiet town of Armero in central Colombia slept, a strange rain started to fall. It was ash that had been spewed into the air by the Nevado del Ruiz, a volcano 46 miles (74 km) away. Scientists had warned that the volcano was due to erupt, but the authorities ignored them. The volcano had been quiet since 1845, and that seemed unlikely to change. Even when the eruption began, the volcano was hidden in clouds, so no one could see it. Most of the 22,000 residents of Armero went to bed without realizing that anything was wrong.

The ash rain was followed by a torrent of volcanic mud and melted snow, known as a lahar. The lahar tumbled down the mountain at 30 miles (48 km) per hour and was over 130 feet (40 m) deep. It destroyed everything in its path—including Armero. The mudslide buried 5,000 buildings and killed almost everyone in town in seconds.

◀ The rooftops of Armero are just visible above the mud.

beaches, the coastal region is also home to Colombia's highest mountain range, the Sierra Nevada de Santa Marta. Its two highest peaks are the Cristóbal Colón and Simón Bolívar, named after two of the most important people in Colombia's history. Cristóbal Colón is the Spanish name for the explorer Christopher Columbus, for whom the country is named. Simón Bolívar was the general who led the fight to make Colombia an independent country. Off the coast, the Caribbean islands of San Andrés and Old Providence also belong to Colombia.

Down in the Jungle

Along with its neighbors, Colombia shares part of the world's largest tropical rain forest, the Amazon. The Amazon River itself only skirts about

▲ A food vendor fires up her stove on the waterfront in Cartagena, a popular destination for visitors on the warm Caribbean coast.

▼ A helicopter is the best way to travel through Colombia's densely forested hills.

50 miles (80 km) of Colombia's border in the far south of the country. But the river's tributaries—smaller rivers that flow into the Amazon—extend across the southern half of Colombia. This area is mainly low-lying land that has warm weather and high rainfall all year around. As a result, it is covered in thick, steamy jungle.

The Amazon rain forest is not the wettest part of Colombia, however. That honor goes to the Chocó region in the northwest, towards the border with Panama. Few people live in this area—and one reason is that it is the rainiest place in South America. The regional capital, Quibdó, has an annual rainfall of more than 354 inches (899 cm). That is enough water to cover a two-story house.

▲ Girls play in the rain in the Chocó region, one of the rainiest places in the world.

▼ The Colombian Andes are full of volcanoes, but only seven have been active in the last 500 years.

First Link in the Chain

The northern tip of the Andes Mountains dominates Colombia. Three-quarters of Colombians live on their

WHERE THE ROAD RUNS OUT

The Pan American Highway is sometimes called the longest road in the world. It runs 26,000 miles (41,600 km) from Alaska to the tip of South America in Argentina. At least, that is the idea. In fact, the road is broken on either side of Colombia's border with Panama (*map, right*). This is the Darien Gap (*below*). It is only about 100 miles (160 km) long and 30 miles (50 km) across, but its mountains, rain forest, and swamps have long been passable only by canoe or on foot. Few people have made the journey.

For many years the region was dangerous, because Colombian rebels fighting the government used it as a place to hide. Today, the area is safer. Some people want to finally build a road and rail link. Others argue that the Darien Gap should be left alone. It is one of the wildest regions on Earth and forms a barrier that stops animals from either side from spreading into new territory.

slopes, and most of the big cities, including the capital, Bogotá, are located there. There are three main mountain ranges or *cordilleras*: the Cordillera Occidental (western), Cordillera Central, and Cordillera Oriental (eastern). They meet near Pasto in the south of Colombia, where they join the rest of the Andes.

Between the mountains are two river valleys, the Valle del Cauca (Cauca Valley) and the Valle del Magdalena (Magdalena Valley). Over millions of years,

Geography　　**13**

ash from the many volcanoes in the area has been added to the valleys' soils, making them very rich and fertile.

Bogotá sits on a large plateau to the east of the Magdalena Valley at an elevation of 8,660 feet

▲ The fertile land of Tierradentro, at the southern end of the Magdalena Valley, has been farmed for thousands of years.

(2,640 m). That makes the city higher—but not colder—than some of the ski resorts in North America, including Aspen, Colorado.

Los Llanos

Between the rain forest and the mountains lie *Los Llanos*, the Colombians' word for "the plains." These

CATTLE COUNTRY

One in ten of the world's cattle live in Colombia. Most of them live near the northern coast, but some are herded on Los Llanos, an immense grass plain that covers about one-third of the country. Los Llanos is a remote place; fewer than one million Colombians live there. There are few roads, and cowboys, or *vaqueros*, travel by horse. During the rainy season, however, many routes become impassable even on horseback. For those months, most towns and villages can be reached only by airplane—or by boat.

▲ A team of vaqueros heads out across the flooded Llanos.

vast, almost treeless, grasslands extend into Venezuela. They lie in a huge natural basin that formed around 60 million years ago when the Andes began to rise in the west. Rivers washed soil into the basin, creating a savannah landscape. The area is drained today by the Orinoco River, which is one of South America's longest waterways.

The grasslands cover an area of around 155,000 square miles (250,000 square km) of Colombia, but are home to only 2 percent of the country's population. Although it has a wet rainy season, Los Llanos is very dry for most of the year. There is not enough water in the soil to support many trees or crops—but the grass that grows here has been used for centuries to raise cattle.

Dry Land

Not everywhere in Colombia is regularly lashed with heavy rain. The Guajira Peninsula, which sticks out onto the Caribbean at the northernmost tip of Colombia, is a desert. The combination of mountains to the south and ocean to the north keeps the rain in the area to a minimum. The desert is the driest place in Colombia—but not the hottest. That record belongs to the Maracaibo Basin in Norte de Santander on the border with Venezuela.

▼ Workers shovel rock salt at a mine in the Guajira Peninsula. The salt is dried in the sun before being processed for people to eat.

Eyes
in the
Trees

THE FORESTS OF COLOMBIA are home to some very unusual monkeys. While other monkeys curl up for a sleep in the branches each evening, that is when the night monkey comes out to feed. No other monkey in the world is active in the dark. The night monkey has supersenses, including huge eyes that can see even in faint light. Night monkeys also have more sensitive noses than any other monkeys, so they can sniff out ripe fruits and flowers in the darkness.

Colombia's forests hold many other wonders. In rainy areas lush forests grow with moss-covered trees. Brightly colored birds, such as the trogon, fly overhead. In drier regions, tortoises, iguana lizards, and armadillos are also common.

◀ Three night monkeys peer into the darkness. Unfortunately these cute creatures are in danger of extinction.

A MULTITUDE OF HABITATS

Ten percent of all the world's plant and animal species live in Colombia, although it covers less than one percent of the world's land area. The great variety of life is due in part to the many different habitats found in the country. The map opposite shows Colombia's vegetation zones—what grows where in the country. Each zone is home to a distinct type of wildlife.

Colombia's forest habitats have been undisturbed for many millions of years, which has given wildlife a chance to evolve into a wealth of different species. Colombia has at least 350 mammal species, including 15 percent of the world's primates, and approximately 1,800 bird species, which is almost 20 percent of the world's total. Some 20,000 of the plants that grow in Colombia are found nowhere else.

▶ The Orinoco crocodile is so rare that babies are now bred at a special center to be released into the wild.

Species at Risk

Colombia's animals and plants are coming under threat as the human population grows. Logging is a major danger in lowland areas and many mountain forests have been replaced by pastures for cattle. Few people live in the rolling grasslands because of the poor quality of the soil in the area. Most of Colombia's farms are in the fertile mountain valleys. Among the fields and cities there is not much room left for wildlife in the highly populated mountains.

Species at risk include:
> Colombian weasel
> Cotton-top tamarin (monkey)
> Giant armadillo
> Giant otter
> Mountain tapir (mammal)
> Naked-tailed armadillo
> Orinoco crocodile
> Pacarana (rodent)
> Sapphire-bellied hummingbird
> Variegated spider monkey

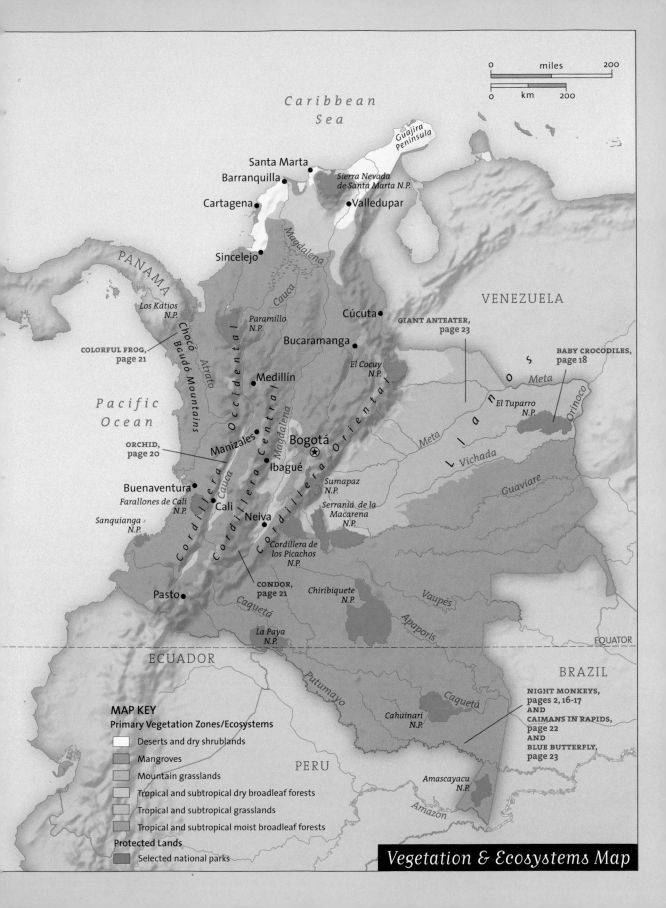

Caribbean
Sea

0   miles   200

0   km   200

*Guajira
Peninsula*

Santa Marta

Barranquilla

Magdalena

*Sierra Nevada
de Santa Marta N.P.*

Valledupar

Cartagena

PANAMA

Sincelejo

Cauca

VENEZUELA

Cúcuta

*Los Kátios
N.P.*

*Paramillo
N.P.*

**GIANT ANTEATER,
page 23**

**COLORFUL FROG,
page 21**

Bucaramanga

**BABY CROCODILES,
page 18**

*El Cocuy
N.P.*

Meta

Orinoco

Medellín

*El Tuparro
N.P.*

*Pacific
Ocean*

**ORCHID,
page 20**

Manizales

Magdalena

Bogotá

Meta

Vichada

Ibagué

Cauca

Guaviare

Buenaventura

*Sumapaz
N.P.*

*Farallones de Cali
N.P.*

Cali

*Serranía de la
Macarena
N.P.*

*Sanquianga
N.P.*

Neiva

*Cordillera de
los Picachos
N.P.*

**CONDOR,
page 21**

*Chiribiquete
N.P.*

Vaupés

Pasto

Caquetá

Apaporis

*La Paya
N.P.*

EQUATOR

ECUADOR

BRAZIL

Putumayo

**NIGHT MONKEYS,
pages 2, 16–17
AND
CAIMANS IN RAPIDS,
page 22
AND
BLUE BUTTERFLY,
page 23**

Caquetá

*Cahuinari
N.P.*

PERU

MAP KEY

Primary Vegetation Zones/Ecosystems

Deserts and dry shrublands

Mangroves

Mountain grasslands

Tropical and subtropical dry broadleaf forests

Tropical and subtropical grasslands

Tropical and subtropical moist broadleaf forests

Protected Lands

Selected national parks

*Amascayacu
N.P.*

Amazon

Vegetation & Ecosystems Map

*Chocó
Baudó Mountains*

Atrato

Cordillera Occidental

Cordillera Central

Cordillera Oriental

Cauca

Llanos

Lost Forests

Colombia is so fertile that if its countryside were left alone by people and all farm animals were removed, it would soon be almost completely covered again in forests. Even Los Llanos would have areas of thin woodland. Only the dry, desert areas and the tops of the mountains would not have trees.

Thousands of years ago, that's just how Colombia was. Since then, however, people have cleared trees to make way for fields and plantations. Some of the Los Llanos grassland has been turned into pasture for cattle. Only the steepest slopes of the Andes mountains still have the original forest. These forests are renowned for their great variety of orchids. Most of the 30,000 orchid species that live in Colombia grow there, although some orchids are also found in the sandy dunes of the Guajira Desert.

▲ Colombia's forests are full of elaborate orchid flowers. More orchids grow in Colombia than anywhere else on Earth.

Down in the Jungle

The largest areas of forest in Colombia are the jungles of the Amazon Basin in the south and the rain forest of the wet Chocó region. The Chocó also has long stretches of mangrove swamp, which lie along the Pacific coast and also around the mouth of the Atrato River. The swamps of the Atrato are home to the Caribbean manatee.

Inland, the Chocó forest has 450 of Colombia's 1,800 bird species. The jungle is also home to howler monkeys, raccoons, deer, and peccaries. Large rodents, such as agoutis, pacas, and capybaras, live in the swampy areas.

Prowling Hunters

The forest is good hunting ground for Colombia's largest predators. The rosette pattern on a jaguar's fur keeps the big cat hidden in the dappled light under the trees. Colombia is also home to the harpy eagle, the world's largest eagle. It swoops through the forest to snatch monkeys and sloths from the treetops.

The largest hunter is the black caiman. *Caiman* is the South American name for "alligator." Black caimans grow to 20 feet (6 m) long and live in rivers and swamps. They also occasionally swim a little way out to sea.

FATAL FROG

One of the world's most dangerous animals lives in the Chocó. The poison-arrow frog doesn't look dangerous: It is tiny and has beautiful bright colors. But the poison in its skin is so powerful that just touching the frog can cause pain. If the poison gets into a cut it can kill a person. The frog got its name because the Chocó Indians carefully collect the poison and put it on the tips of the arrows they use when hunting. Without their diet of toxic rain forest insects, however, the frogs are completely harmless. Some people even keep them as pets.

▶ The frog's bright colors warn animals to stay away.

▼ Andean condors have the largest wings of any bird, which they use to ride warm air currents among high peaks.

The tributaries of the Amazon River in the south of Colombia are home to an altogether different type of caiman. Cuvier's dwarf caiman is the smallest kind of crocodilian in the world. It grows to just 5 feet (1.5 m) long. Black caimans snap up fish and water birds, but dwarf caimans swim in fast-flowing streams where they feed on shellfish.

The rivers that cross Los Llanos flow into the Orinoco River, and are home to the rare Orinoco crocodile. This species and the caimans have long been hunted for their skins—and not just in Colombia. It is estimated that the number of caimans in South America has fallen by 99 percent in the last hundred years.

▼ Black caimans wait in river rapids with their mouths open ready to snatch unsuspecting fish.

Rare Bear

One of the largest mammal species in Colombia is the rarely seen spectacled bear. The only bear species living in South America, it hides in thick vegetation high in the Andes. It is named for the pale rings around its eyes, which look like a pair of glasses.

The bear lives in the mountain forests, surviving on a range of foods from nuts and honey to baby deer. The forests are damp and thick with vegetation such

TOOTHLESS GIANT

The forests, grassland, and swamps of Colombia are home to one of the weirdest-looking of all animals: the giant anteater. It is easily recognizable by what looks like a long nose. In fact the "nose" is its mouth, and contains a tongue that is almost as long as the rest of its whole body. Such a large tongue is vital: An anteater needs to eat a lot of ants. The animal uses its forearms and claws to tear open ants' nests and termite mounds, and then uses its sticky tongue to lick up the insects. The anteater flicks its tongue in and out of its mouth up to 150 times a minute. A 6-foot (1.8-m) giant anteater eats 30,000 insects a day!

▲ An orphaned baby anteater is fed milk from a bottle.

as vinelike lianas and fleshy bromeliads—plants that grow high up in trees. Large plants include rubber trees and giant bamboo.

The spectacled bear also sometimes moves higher up the mountains, where the forest is replaced by vegetation called *páramo*. This is unique to the Andes and is a mix of grasses and plants called *frailejón*, which are large bushes with hairy leaves.

Flashes of Color

The tropical forests are filled with color as butterflies and birds, such as resplendent quetzals, toucans, and macaws (large parrots), fly among the branches. Los Llanos also attract many birds. Most are waterbirds, such as herons, flamingoes, and egrets. They arrive after the start of the rainy season, which floods the grasslands with shallow pools.

▼ Colombia's forests are full of thousands of different types of colorful butterflies. Many, like this one, are still to be identified by biologists.

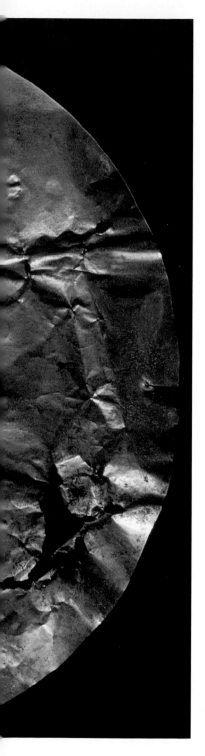

Legends
of
Gold

WHEN SPANISH EXPLORERS arrived in what is now Colombia in 1500, they heard tales of people made of gold. Over time, the stories became the legend of El Dorado: "the golden one." For decades, the hope of finding fabulous wealth drew Spanish adventurers to Colombia.

The people the Spaniards met were not wealthy—but their past had its own legends and mysteries. We know very little about the life of early Colombians. One of the biggest mysteries is at San Augustín high up the Magdalena Valley. Some 500 stones stand near the village, carved with the faces of eagles, jaguars, snakes, frogs, and humans. The stones, which are up to 20 feet (7 m) tall, are centuries old. Perhaps they were used in religious rituals. But no one knows their precise purpose or who carved them.

◀ **A gold mask made by the Calima people from what is now Colombia's Pacific coast**

ANCIENT PEOPLES

Colombia is the overland gateway to South America. The earliest inhabitants of the continent traveled through present-day Colombia as they migrated from North America south. However, Colombia never supported large civilizations like the Inca of Peru or the Aztec and Maya of Mexico.

Archaeologists have found evidence that ancient peoples lived near to Colombia's rivers. The main

▲ **The mysterious carvings at San Augustín**

site so far discovered is San Augustín, near the Magdalena River, but the statues there still guard many of their secrets. We do know that sculptures were carved around 1,000 years ago by people who lived by growing crops like corn and yucca, and gathering berries. Archaeologists suggest that they lived comfortably because they had time to make the beautiful stone carvings. But whoever they were, these early Colombians had left the area long before the Europeans arrived in the 16th century.

Time line

This chart shows the approximate dates of events in the history of Colombia from before the arrival of European explorers to the present day.

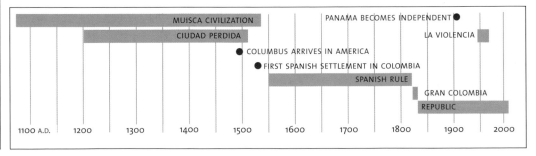

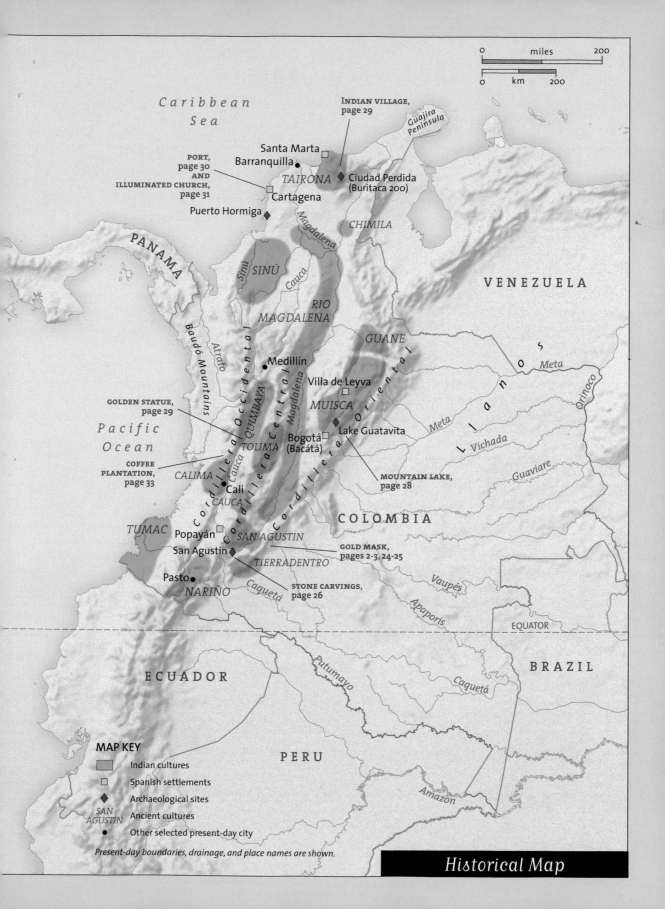

Caribbean
Sea

INDIAN VILLAGE,
page 29

*Guajira
Peninsula*

Santa Marta
Barranquilla

PORT,
page 30
AND
ILLUMINATED CHURCH,
page 31

TAIRONA

Ciudad Perdida
(Buritaca 200)

Cartagena

Puerto Hormiga

Magdalena

CHIMILA

PANAMA

Sinú

SINÚ

Cauca

RIO
MAGDALENA

VENEZUELA

Baudó Mountains

Atrato

Cordillera Occidental

Medillín

GUANE

L l a n o s

Meta

GOLDEN STATUE,
page 29

Pacific
Ocean

Cauca

QUIMBAYA

TOLIMA

Cordillera Central

Magdalena

Villa de Leyva

MUISCA

Lake Guatavita

Cordillera Oriental

Meta

Orinoco

Vichada

COFFEE
PLANTATION,
page 33

CALIMA

Bogotá
(Bacatá)

Guaviare

Cali

CAUCA

MOUNTAIN LAKE,
page 28

COLOMBIA

TUMAC

Popayán

SAN AGUSTIN

Vaupés

San Agustín

GOLD MASK,
pages 2-3, 24-25

Cordillera Central

Cordillera Oriental

Pasto

TIERRADENTRO

Caquetá

STONE CARVINGS,
page 26

Apaporis

NARIÑO

EQUATOR

ECUADOR

Putumayo

Caquetá

BRAZIL

PERU

Amazon

MAP KEY

Indian cultures

Spanish settlements

Archaeological sites

*SAN
AGUSTIN* Ancient cultures

Other selected present-day city

Present-day boundaries, drainage, and place names are shown.

Historical Map

scale: 0 — miles — 200
0 — km — 200

The First Colombians

The first people arrived in Colombia about 20,000 years ago. Little is known about their lives because they did not leave much evidence behind. Around 12,000 years ago, new groups settled on the plateau that is now the site of Bogotá and set up homes elsewhere in the valley of the Magdalena River. These groups grew into a civilization known as the Chibcha.

When the first Spanish explorers arrived in Colombia 500 years ago, they met the Muisca, also known as the Chibcha after their language. They also came across people from seven other pre-Columbian civilizations—peoples who lived in the Americas before Christopher

A GOLDEN POND

On the eastern slope of the Magdalena Valley is a round, deep lake with a special history. The Muisca used Lake Guatavita to hold a spectacular ritual. They covered their chief from head to foot in gold dust. He then plunged into the water, washing off the gold as an offering to the gods. The Muisca also threw jewels and other precious objects into the lake during the ceremony.

The ceremony probably gave rise to the legend of the golden man, known to the Spaniards as El Dorado. Spanish expeditions traveled up the Magdalena River to find El Dorado. They fought their way through dense

▲ According to legend, Lake Guatavita is full of gold and jewels from Chibcha ceremonies.

jungle to find the man made of gold. In 1580, Spanish treasure hunters tried to drain the lake by blasting a hole in the bank. They failed to make more than a notch in the cliff. The contents of the lake bottom remain a mystery.

Columbus crossed the Atlantic.

The Muisca were the most advanced of these peoples. From their homeland in the high plateaus of the Cordillera Occidental, they rose to become the dominant power in Colombia in about A.D. 700.

We know quite a lot about the Muisca. Like the Inca of Peru, they worshiped the sun and performed human sacrifices. But they did not build huge cities like the Inca. The Muisca lived in villages of mud-covered houses built from cane. They grew corn and potatoes and traded with other groups.

The Lost City

North of the Andes, in the Sierra Nevada de Santa Marta, lies the Ciudad Perdida or "Lost City." This mysterious place is one of the largest pre-Columbian

◀ This golden statue was made by people living along the Cauca River in a valley west of the main Chibcha territory.

▼ In the Sierra Nevada de Santa Marta in northern Colombia, the Kogi still live much as their pre-Columbian ancestors did. The Kogi were never conquered by the Spaniards.

cities so far discovered in South America. The Tayrona people built it on the northern slopes of the high mountains. Archaeologists believe the city was used between the 11th and 15th centuries A.D. and was home to up to 4,000 people. Spanish invaders killed most of the Tayrona in the early 1500s, and the jungle gradually swallowed the city. Ciudad Perdida lay hidden in the forest until it was rediscovered in 1975.

A Spanish Land

Explorers from Spain first visited the Colombian coast in 1500. After Columbus' voyage eight years earlier, they were eager to investigate the "New World." They did not find much interesting in Colombia, and soon

CARTAGENA

Cartagena was founded in 1533 and soon became Spain's most important port. All the gold, silver, and precious stones shipped from South America back to Spain passed through Cartagena. The port was also an entry point for slaves from Africa.

Cartagena became hugely wealthy, with splendid mansions and public buildings. Its wealth made it a target for frequent pirate attacks. In one attack in 1586, the town was destroyed by fire. The citizens rebuilt the town with a thick wall, but attackers still came. British ships laid siege to the town in 1741,

▲ The fortress of Santo Domingo still guards the modern city of Cartagena.

demanding all its gold. Much to their surprise, the city withstood the siege without surrendering. Today, Cartagena's old colonial streets are popular tourist attractions.

moved on. Another 25 years passed before the Spanish built a permanent base on the north coast: Santa Marta. Today, it is the oldest town in Colombia.

The first Spanish settlers were obsessed with finding treasure. In 1536, Gonzalo Jiménez de Quesada led an expedition inland along the Magdalena Valley. He met and easily defeated the Muisca. In 1538, Spanish raiders looted the Muisca's capital Bacátá, stealing its gold and 230 emeralds. Shortly after, the Spaniards built their own city beside the old capital. The new city soon became known by a Spanish version of the Muisca name: Bogotá.

▲ The Church of San Pedro Claver in Cartagena was built in 1603. Its altar contains the skull of a priest who cared for thousands of African slaves. The town was the largest slave market in the Caribbean.

▼ Early Colombian peoples used emeralds for jewelry, and the country is still the world's main source of the stones.

New Granada

In 1550 the Spanish king organized the north of South America into a huge colony called New Granada, which stretched from Ecuador to Venezuela. It included the settlements along the Colombian coast. Few Spaniards lived in

LOSING PANAMA

When Colombia became independent, its territory included the Isthmus of Panama. The United States wanted to build a canal to join the Atlantic and Pacific oceans. That would cut the voyage between the east and west coasts of North America, and improve U.S. trade and naval strength.

Colombia refused to sell Panama, so in 1903 the United States encouraged a Panamanian rebellion that ended in independence. Panama gave the United States a 10-mile-wide (16-km) strip of land where the Panama Canal was opened in 1914.

the southern forests, which became part of the colony of Peru.

The Spanish merchants of New Granada grew rich from trading gold and jewels—and slaves. They brought Africans to work in the mines. Colombia was ruled by Spain for more than 250 years.

▼ A statue of Simón Bolívar, the liberator of Colombia, stands in Washington, D.C.

Independence!

By the late 1700s, people in South America felt little connection with their Spanish rulers. They wanted to govern themselves. In November 1811, Cartagena declared its independence from Spain; Bogotá followed. In 1815 Spanish soldiers arrived to reclaim control, but Spain had been weakened by wars in Europe. It fought for New Granada until August 1819, when the Venezuelan general Simón Bolívar defeated the Spanish forces at Boyacá in the mountains north of Bogotá.

Battle for Control

Bolívar set up a country called Gran Colombia, which was made up of what are now Colombia, Ecuador, Panama, and Venezuela. The general then headed south, where other countries were fighting the Spanish for independence. Without him, Gran

SIMON BOLIVAR
THE LIBERATOR

"THE VIOLENCE"

Colombia has often been a dangerous place. One of the most violent periods, in the middle of the 20th century, is known simply as La Violencia. Fighting broke out in 1948 following the assassination of Jorge Eliécer Gaitán, the leader of the Liberal Party. Fighting broke out between Liberal gangs and their opponents, the Conservatives. The many revenge attacks amounted to a civil war that lasted until 1958. About 200,000 people were killed. Thousands more fled the massacres that took place in the countryside. The bloody era only ended when the Liberals and Conservatives agreed to share power.

Colombia fell apart. By 1835, Colombia had become a separate country.

From the start there was a battle to control the country. Conservatives wanted the Catholic Church to be closely linked to a powerful central government. Liberals wanted to keep the church out of politics, and to make the country a federation of states.

The conflict has never really ended. It has caused many periods of violence and civil war. Colombia enjoyed its longest period of peace in the early 20th century, when it became a leading producer of bananas and coffee. However, turmoil returned later in the century, when rebel forces and criminal gangs took control of large parts of the country.

▼ Coffee grows on the lush slopes of the Andes. Colombia is the world's second-largest coffee producer, after Brazil. Colombian coffee is famous all over the world.

A Mix
of
People

COLOMBIA'S PEOPLE ARE AS VARIED as its landscape. Colombians are descended from three ethnic groups—the pre-Columbian Indians, African people forced to work as slaves, and European settlers. Their faces reflect this mixture of heritages. Nearly 60 percent of Colombians are *mestizos*. They are descended from Indian women who gave birth to children fathered by Spanish conquerors and settlers.

As a legacy of the slave trade, 26 percent of Colombians—11 million people—have African heritage. Brazil is the only American nation with a higher proportion. Most Afro-Colombians live near the coasts. The remaining Indian groups live in isolation in remote inland parts of the country.

◀ The Sibundoy are an Indian group from the hills near Ecuador. Despite their remote location, they have economic, cultural, and political interactions with other Colombians.

URBAN AND RURAL POPULATION

During the middle part of the 20th century, Colombia changed from a rural to an urban country as large numbers of people moved to the cities to find work. Today, three-quarters of Colombians live in cities. Colombia is unusual in South America because it has so many large cities: Four have more than a million residents. The largest city is the capital, Bogotá, where seven million people live. On the other hand, Los Llanos, and the Amazonian forest, which covers half of the country, are almost deserted. The most densely populated parts of countryside are the mountainous areas where coffee grows.

▶ A suburb of Medellín, Colombia's second largest city, has a cable-car metro system.

Common Spanish Phrases

The official language of Colombia is Spanish. Colombians are very proud of their language, which some consider is the purest form of Spanish in Latin America. The government has passed laws to try to protect the language. Here are some common Spanish phrases. Give them a try:

Hello	Hola (hoh lah)
Goodbye	Adiós (ah dee os)
How's it going?	Qué tal? (keh tahl)
See you soon	Hasta luego (ha stah loo eh go)
No	No
Yes	Sí

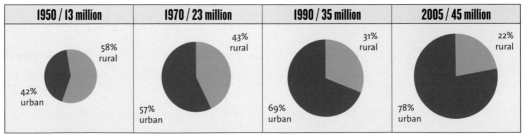

1950 / 13 million	1970 / 23 million	1990 / 35 million	2005 / 45 million
58% rural / 42% urban	43% rural / 57% urban	31% rural / 69% urban	22% rural / 78% urban

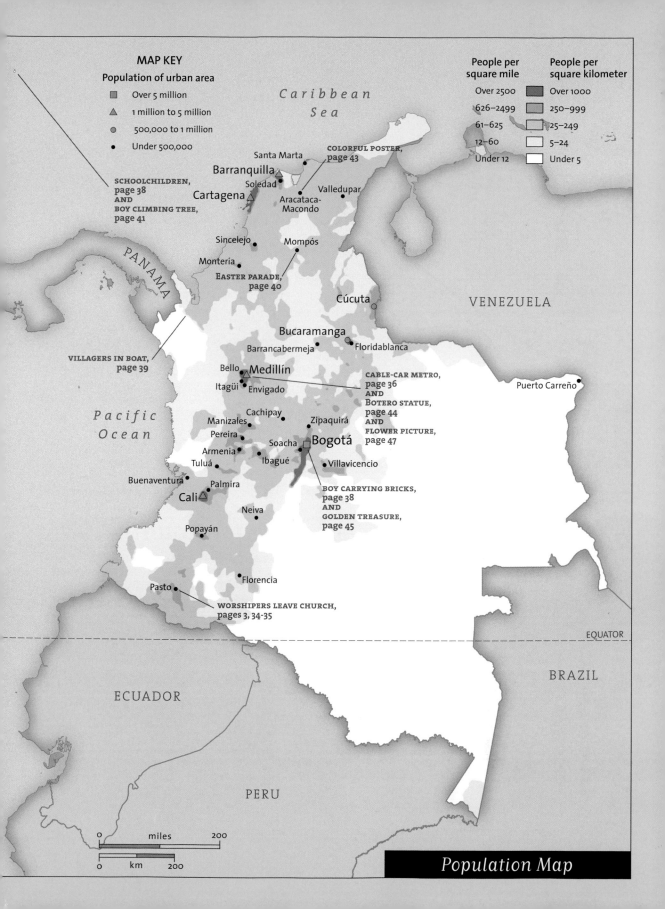

MAP KEY

Population of urban area

■ Over 5 million

▲ 1 million to 5 million

● 500,000 to 1 million

• Under 500,000

People per square mile	People per square kilometer
Over 2500	Over 1000
626–2499	250–999
61–625	25–249
12–60	5–24
Under 12	Under 5

Caribbean Sea

SCHOOLCHILDREN, page 38 AND BOY CLIMBING TREE, page 41

Santa Marta

Barranquilla

Soledad

COLORFUL POSTER, page 43

Cartagena

Aracataca-Macondo

Valledupar

PANAMA

Sincelejo

Mompós

Montería

EASTER PARADE, page 40

Cúcuta

VENEZUELA

Bucaramanga

Barrancabermeja

Floridablanca

VILLAGERS IN BOAT, page 39

Bello

Medellín

Itagüí

Envigado

CABLE-CAR METRO, page 36 AND BOTERO STATUE, page 44 AND FLOWER PICTURE, page 47

Pacific Ocean

Cachipay

Manizales

Zipaquirá

Pereira

Soacha

Bogotá

Armenia

Ibagué

Villavicencio

Tuluá

Buenaventura

Palmira

BOY CARRYING BRICKS, page 38 AND GOLDEN TREASURE, page 45

Cali

Neiva

Puerto Carreño

Popayán

Florencia

Pasto

WORSHIPERS LEAVE CHURCH, pages 3, 34-35

EQUATOR

BRAZIL

ECUADOR

PERU

	miles	
0		200
0	km	200

Population Map

▲ Schoolchildren take a break at a Colombian school.

▼ Many Colombian children have to work in adult jobs to raise money for their families.

City Learning

For children who live in Colombia's cities, going to school is a lot like going to school anywhere else. School is compulsory between the ages of five and sixteen. In areas with a large population, schools sometimes operate a shift system to fit all the students in. The younger children attend in the morning and the older children in the afternoon.

When students have finished elementary and junior high school, most go to high school until they are 18 or 19. For those who graduate, there are more than 130 colleges to choose from. However, college is too expensive for 80 percent of Colombians.

In the Country

For children living in the countryside, it is a lot harder to get a good education. Some children have to help their parents work in the fields. For children in remote places like the Chocó and Los Llanos, the nearest school might be far from their home. There is no public transportation, and no school buses, so the only way for the children to get to school is to walk—even if it's miles away.

There are other ways for children in remote areas to learn. In the 1950s, Colombia was the first country in South America to teach lessons by radio. Since the early 1980s it has also broadcast regular educational TV shows, aimed both at students and at adults who have had no schooling. TV and radio lessons have helped reduce the number of Colombians who cannot read from around 50 percent in the 1950s to only 7 percent today.

▼ There are few roads in the dense Chocó rain forest, so villagers travel by river boat.

A Catholic Nation

At the heart of Colombian society is the Roman Catholic Church. Christianity was brought to the country by Spanish missionaries almost 500 years ago. Churches are everywhere. There is even a cathedral carved entirely out of salt in a mine in Zipaquirá.

Catholicism is the largest religion of Colombia and more than 90 percent of Colombians are Catholics. Most of Colombia's public holidays are saint's days and

other religious festivals. Most families go to church on Sunday, and children are usually christened as infants and confirmed later. However, more Colombians are now joining new types of churches.

Loving Rhythm

Colombians love to dance and listen to music. Two of the most popular types of music, the *cumbia* and *vallenato*, come from when Colombia was home to many African slaves and Spanish slave-owners. The music combines Spanish melodies and African rhythms brought by the slaves when they arrived at Cartagena.

In some Andean countries, such as Peru or Bolivia, music is influenced by the music of pre-Columbian peoples. In Colombia, however, music is played on a mix of European, African, and Indian instruments. The tune of the vallenato is played on an accordion, but the rhythm comes from a *caja* drum, which is like a bongo, and a *guacharaca*, an Indian instrument made of a palm stick that is scraped with a metal fork.

▲ **Nearly the whole population of the small town of Mompos carries palm leaves in a parade to mark Palm Sunday in Holy Week.**

The cumbia's lively mix of guitars, accordion, bass, drums, and flutes has spread beyond Colombia to the rest of Latin America. It is still played in villages by local bands, but now it is so popular that you can listen to cumbia bands in cities across the world.

Colombian music is meant for dancing. Children and adults often hold public dance performances and competitions during village festivals.

Family Food

Meal time is a highlight of the day for many Colombians. It is a chance for families and friends to come together to eat.

Lunch is traditionally the largest meal of the day, but modern life is too busy for many people in the cities to enjoy a big meal except on weekends. During the week, people might eat snack meals instead. The most popular are *empanadas*, a pastry filled with either meat or chicken and vegetables. Another popular snack is corn griddle pancakes,

◀ Coconuts are a favorite food—but not everyone picks their own like this boy on the Caribbean coast.

or *arepas. Buñuelos*—a deep-fried ball of corn flour and cheese—are another favorite. Fresh fruit is a popular dessert. Mango, pineapple, and passion fruit are squeezed to make juice.

Colombian dishes vary between regions. On the coast, people eat a lot more fish than in the highlands, where meat dishes are common. In the south, toward Ecuador, people cook with potatoes. In the rest of the country, most dishes are served with rice, corn, plantains (unsweet bananas), and *yucca* (cassava roots).

▲ Empanadas can contain a wide variety of fillings.

SHAKIRA ROCKS!

▲ A little girl from Bogotá plays with a Shakira doll.

Shakira Isabel Mebarak Ripoli is better known to hundreds of thousands of fans simply as Shakira. Colombia's most successful pop singer, she has become popular around the globe. Shakira danced and sang from an early age, and recorded her first album in 1991 at just 14 years old. Her career took off and by 1995 she was a huge star across Latin America. Her popularity also grew in the United States, where she won a Grammy award for her performance in the first Spanish-language edition of *MTV Unplugged*.

Shakira's career has gone from strength to strength. In August 2000 she was crowned favorite international artist at the MTV Video Music Awards. She realized that she was too popular to perform only in Spanish, so she learned English and now sings in both languages. Shakira is the only Colombian star to get to Number 1 on the U.S. Billboard Chart—with "Hips Don't Lie" in 2006.

Coffee is the most popular drink for adults, not just at breakfast but throughout the day. Children drink *agua de panela*, which is brown sugar in water.

Magical Books

Colombia has provided the inspiration for one of the world's leading novelists, the Nobel-prize winner Gabriel García Márquez. His 1967 novel *Cien Años de Soledad* (*One Hundred Years of Solitude*) began a new era in Hispanic American novels. It is one of the most popular books ever written in Spanish. Another of García Márquez's novels, *Amor En Los Tiempos de Cólera* (*Love in the Time of Cholera*), was made into a

▲ A poster urges the people of Aracataca, the birthplace of Gabriel García Márquez, to vote to change the town's name. The town's new name included the name Macondo, the fictional setting of García Márquez's most popular novel, *One Hundred Years of Solitude*.

FERNANDO BOTERO

I t's easy to tell a painting or a sculpture by Colombia's most famous artist, Fernando Botero. Round, flat, and very large faces stare out of the paintings. The bronze sculptures are also rounded, smooth, and larger than life. The figures of people and animals have almost a cartoon quality.

Botero was born in Medellín in 1932 and first exhibited his paintings in Bogotá, at age 19. He paints scenes of daily life in small towns, inspired by his childhood, and often also includes the Colombian flag. Botero moved to Paris in 1973 and took up sculpture. His distinctive forms are particularly popular for outdoor display in squares or parks. They can be seen in New York and Chicago and across Europe. A whole square in Medellín is devoted to his sculptures.

▶ A Fernando Botero sculpture in Medellín

movie set in Cartagena. Many of García Márquez's novels use a style called magical realism. Unbelievable things happen, such as someone floating away into the sky, but they are treated by the characters as if they are completely normal. García Márquez also uses his work to criticize the Colombian government and its failure to solve Colombia's social problems.

Ancient and Modern

Bogotá's Museo del Oro (Museum of Gold) holds more than 34,000 pieces of pre-Columbian art. They include a replica of a gold raft called the *Balsa Muisca* used by the Chibcha people for religious ceremonies. The highlight of the museum is a whole room full of golden objects, named for El Dorado.

Many historic treasures were sent abroad by the Spaniards. Today, the artifacts are kept within the country. Colombia's main cultural exports are TV shows that are watched across the Spanish-speaking world. One very popular type of show is the *telenovela*, or soap opera. Every year, Colombian television studios produce dozens of telenovelas.

UGLY ORIGINAL

One of the most successful recent U.S. TV shows is based on a Colombian soap opera. The series was named *Yo Soy Betty, La Fea*, or "I am Betty, the ugly one." In English, it is known as *Ugly Betty*. The Colombian original was broadcast between 1999 and 2001. It told the story of a very smart but plain-looking woman who works for a fashion magazine. Betty is treated badly by the other staff, who are more stylish and beautiful, but eventually her brains make her an invaluable member of the team.

▲ Ana Maria Orozco starred as Betty.

NATIONAL HOLIDAYS

Colombia has many public holidays to celebrate religious festivals and nonreligious occasions such as independence. Every town and city also has its own special holidays.

An unusual festival is held in Pasto during the first week of January. On Día de Negritos (Day of the Black Ones), on January 5, the local boys chase the girls with dark make-up and try to blacken their hands and faces. On the next day, Fiesta de Los Blanquitos (Festival of the White Ones), the boys attempt to throw flour and white powder over the girls.

JANUARY 1	New Year's Day
JANUARY 6	Epiphany
MARCH/APRIL	Holy Week (including Easter)
MAY 1	Labor Day
MAY/JUNE	Corpus Christi
JUNE	Sacred Heart
JULY 20	Independence Day
AUGUST 7	Battle of Boyacá Day
AUGUST 15	Assumption Day
OCTOBER 12	Columbus Day
NOVEMBER 1	All Saints Day
NOVEMBER 11	Independence of Cartagena
DECEMBER 8	Immaculate Conception Day
DECEMBER 25	Christmas Day

Crazy for Sports

Soccer is the most popular sport for Colombians to play and watch. The national team is usually one of the strongest in South America and often qualifies for World Cup Finals and Pan-American tournaments. The team is known for its exciting style. The former national goalkeeper, René Higuita, used to clear the ball from his goal with a risky but powerful back flip called the scorpion kick.

Bullfighting was introduced to Colombia by the Spaniards. Most cities have a bullring. Matadors—bullfighters—come from around the world to show off their skills.

Tejo is a traditional game in rural villages. It is a little like horseshoes, but competitors throw heavy metal plates at a clay target on the ground. The center of the target is filled with packets of gunpowder, so it explodes when a plate hits it.

Riding High

Colombia is the only place in South America where cycling is popular. The steep mountain roads of the Colombian Andes are perfect for

SOCCER TRAGEDY

Soccer is Colombia's number one sport, but one fan took his support to a tragic degree. In 1994, the national team was knocked out of the World Cup when it lost to the hosts, the United States. Colombia lost after defender Andres Escobar scored in his own team's goal by mistake. Back home, the defender was shot dead by a angry fan after a brawl in a bar.

▲ Two fans arrange flowers in a memorial to Andres Escobar, the murdered Colombian soccer star.

cyclists who want to train to compete in the world's leading race, the Tour de France, which has a course through the mountains. In 2007 Colombian cyclist Mauricio Soler was crowned "King of the Mountains" as the most successful hill cyclist in that year's Tour de France.

▼ Colombian cyclist Ivan Parra heads for victory in a stage of the Giro d'Italia in 2005.

Colombia has its own cycle race, the Vuelta a Colombia, or Tour of Colombia. It covers 765 miles (1,233 km) of some of the most difficult terrain in Colombia. The race started in 1951, and cyclists consider it one of the toughest races in the world.

The Road
to
Recovery

THE START OF THE 21ST CENTURY saw Colombia's fortunes improve. The new president, Alvaro Uribe Velez, continues to reform Colombia. He is attempting to restore peace by tackling the rebel groups that have fought against the government for the last 40 years.

With financial aid from the United States, his government continued Plan Colombia, a long-running program to rid the country of the gangs, or cartels, that produce illegal drugs for sale around the world.

The chance of long-term peace has begun a boom in Colombia's economy. The illegal drug trade is less likely to cause problems for legal businesses. Today, Colombia is growing rich from regular industries, such as farming, banking, and tourism.

◀ **A crop-dusting plane sprays chemicals to kill the plants being grown to make illegal drugs. The spraying program is part of the government's Plan Colombia.**

LOCAL GOVERNMENT

Colombia is divided into 32 *departamentos* (departments). However, the city of Bogotá has special status and is run as a separate capital district.

A department is similar to a U.S. state. Each department has a governor and an assembly of lawmakers. There are elections every four years, but the sitting department governor is not allowed to run for re-election. Departments are represented at the national level by at least two members of Congress.

The departments are further divided into smaller counties called *municipios* (municipalities). There are a total of 1,119 *municipios* in Colombia. Each one is run by an elected mayor and council.

▶ **An oil storage site sits on top of a hill in central Colombia. Oil is an important export: There are large supplies in the Colombian Andes and Los Llanos.**

Trading Partners

Colombia's main trading partner is the United States. It exports a wide variety of agricultural crops, such as coffee, bananas, and cut flowers, as well as meat, and natural resources, such as petroleum oil and emeralds. Colombia imports most of its industrial equipment, chemicals, metals, and transportation equipment.

Country	Percent Colombia exports
United States	40.0%
European Union	13.3%
Venezuela	9.9%
Ecuador	6.2%
All others combined	30.6%

Country	Percent Colombia imports
United States	28.3%
Mexico	8.3%
China	7.6%
Brazil	6.5%
All others combined	49.3%

Caribbean Sea

VENEZUELA

PANAMA

Pacific Ocean

ECUADOR

PERU

BRAZIL

Riohacha
Santa Marta
Barranquilla
ATLÁNTICO
Cartagena
MAGDALENA
LA GUAJIRA
Valledupar
CESAR
Sincelejo
Monteria
SUCRE
CÓRDOBA
BOLÍVAR
NORTE DE SANTANDER
Cúcuta
Bucaramanga

REBEL SOLDIER IN TRAINING, page 53

PANNING FOR GOLD, page 57

ANTIOQUIA
Medellín
SANTANDER
Arauca
ARAUCA
CASANARE
Puerto Carreño
Quibdó
CHOCÓ
CALDAS
Manizales
RISARALDA
Pereira
Armenia
QUINDÍO
Ibagué
CUNDINAMARCA
Tunja
BOYACÁ
Yopal
Bogotá

OIL TANKS ON HILLTOP, page 50

VICHADA

VALLE DEL CAUCA
Cali
TOLIMA
Villavicencio

COFFEE BERRIES BEING SORTED, page 55

Puerto Inírida

GIRL WITH CANDLE, page 52

Neiva
HUILA
CAUCA
Popayán
META
San José del Guaviare
GUAINÍA

CROP-DUSTER, pages 3, 48-49

NARIÑO
Pasto
Mocoa
Florencia
PUTUMAYO
GUAVIARE
CAQUETÁ
Mitú
VAUPÉS

EQUATOR

AMAZONAS

Leticia

MAP KEY
⊛ National capital
⊙ Department capital

o   miles   200
o   km   200

▲ A girl takes part in a candle-lit protest for *paz* (peace) in Colombia.

Sustaining Democracy

Colombia is unusual compared with many of its Latin American neighbors. It has a long history of democracy, while they have often been ruled by dictators.

Since Colombia won independence in 1821—first as part of Gran Colombia—its politics have been led by the Conservative and Liberal parties. Power swung between the two, accompanied by violence. In 1958 the two sides brought over a century of conflict to an end. They joined forces as the National Front, which

HOW THE GOVERNMENT WORKS

Colombia is a republic. The president is head of state and is in charge of running the government. He or she is elected every four years and is allowed to hold the office of president for a maximum of two terms. The president appoints a team, or cabinet, of ministers who manage different parts of the government.

Laws are made by the Congress. This has two parts. The House of Representatives has 165 members elected from the departments. The work of the representatives is overseen by the 102 members of the Senate, who are chosen in nationwide elections.

Colombia's highest court is the Supreme Court of Justice. Supreme Court judges are appointed by the president and Congress and serve for a single eight-year term.

GOVERNMENT		
EXECUTIVE	LEGISLATIVE	JUDICIARY
PRESIDENT	SENATE (102 MEMBERS)	SUPREME COURT OF JUSTICE
CABINET OF MINISTERS	HOUSE OF REPRESENTATIVES (165 MEMBERS)	DISTRICT COURTS

governed Colombia until 1974. By then, the country had changed from a rural, agricultural society to an urban, industrial one. However, the problems of poverty and injustice in rural areas, which had been one of the main causes of the power battle, were left still unresolved by the National Front administration.

Taking Control

In the 1970s, the problem arose again. Rebel groups restarted the civil war. The rebels were poor farmers who wanted to have more say over what happened on the land. In the chaos, drug cartels could operate

REBELS IN THE MOUNTAINS

In the last half of the 20th century, Colombia was in an almost constant state of civil war. Rebel groups became active in the remote countryside during the 1970s in response to poverty and unjust land laws. The FARC (Fuerzas Armadas Revolucionarias de Colombia) is the largest group. There are about 10,000 fighters. Some rebels use crime to pay for their weapons. Some trade in drugs while others take hostages and demand ransoms from their families. Colombia is one of the worst kidnapping centers in the world.

▼ A rebel soldier trains in a jungle camp.

INDUSTRY MAP

The largest industries in Colombia are manufacturing, agriculture, and livestock. Mines and oil fields are also important. In the cities, banking and other services generate a lot of wealth. The country's largest employer is the government, which pays hospital workers, school teachers, and soldiers.

Caribbean Sea

0 mi 200

0 km 200

Barranquilla

Cartagena

Cu

Medellín
Ni

Au
Fe

Manizales
E Fe

Bogotá

Pacific
Ocean

Cali

Au Cu

MAP KEY

⚙ Manufacturing center

Coal

Petroleum

Processing plant

Major Mines

Au Gold

Cu Copper   **Fe** Iron ore

E Emeralds   **Ni** Nickel

freely, mainly in the Cauca Valley. The government was unable to stop them from selling drugs all over the world.

In 1990, Colombia's political system was modernized. The first step was to rewrite the constitution. It was a bold move: Colombia had the oldest constitution in South America, dating from 1886. The new constitution allowed minorities, such as pre-Columbian groups and black people, to be represented in Congress for the first time.

The changes seem to have had a positive effect. All Colombia's different peoples began working together to run the country better.

Coffee Center

Colombia is best known for its leading export: coffee. The Colombian hills grow some of the best-quality coffee beans in the world. The country produces one-eighth of the world's total coffee crop. Coffee has transformed the Colombian economy. About one-sixth of all the country's fields are used for coffee. There is even a coffee theme park. The Parque Nacional del Café is located in the Cordillera Central at the heart of coffee country. As well as rides, the park has exhibits about the history of coffee and how a raw coffee berry from a tropical hillside becomes a steaming latte in a coffee shop.

Farming Hard

One-quarter of Colombia's land is used for farming. The variety of landscapes makes it possible to grow a range of crops, many of which are exported. After coffee, bananas are the second most important crop. They are grown, along with cotton and sugarcane, on plantations in the northern region. Other crops include rice, tobacco, corn, and cocoa. Other food products from Colombia are beef from Los Llanos and shrimps from the Atlantic.

Less than one-third of the population are farmers. They often produce only enough for their own family. These small farmers are running out of land because of the spread of larger farms and plantations. They are forced to farm on steeper slopes in the mountains. That causes problems with erosion, when mountainsides are washed away by heavy rains.

▲ Workers sort coffee berries at a plantation near Bogatá. The berries contain the bean used to make the hot drink.

▼ Colombia is one of the world's largest producers of bananas.

MR. COFFEE

Look in the kitchen cupboard. If you find a package of Colombian coffee, the chances are that it will have a small logo featuring a man with a large sombrero and a mule, with the Andes mountains in the background. This is Juan Valdéz, the official symbol of Colombian coffee. He does not exist, and neither does his mule, Conchita. Marketing executives dreamed them up. Since 1981, Juan Valdéz has appeared in advertisements for the National Federation of Coffee Growers of Colombia. He has an important job. Colombia sells $1.6 billion worth of coffee a year. Only Brazil produces more. The coffee advertisements have been so successful that an actor plays a full-time role as Juan Valdéz.

▲ An actor poses as Juan Valdéz, the face of Colombian coffee.

Rich in Minerals

Among the earliest attractions that drew Europeans to Colombia were gold and jewels. During Spanish rule, Colombia produced more gold than any other part of Latin America. Centuries later, Colombia still provides these riches. It produces 90 percent of the world's emeralds and large quantities of gold and platinum.

The dry Guajira Peninsula hides another potentially valuable treasure: coal. The reserves are huge— perhaps 60 percent of South America's coal is there. This coal produces less pollution when it is burned than coals from other parts of the world.

New oil strikes have been made in the northern Llanos region and the Amazon to add to reserves in the mountains. Pipelines have been built to transport petroleum across the Andes to the north coast so it can be loaded onto tankers and exported. Colombia's oil production is about 800,000 barrels a day. The country does not use much of its oil and coal as a source of energy. Nearly 75 percent of Colombia's electricity comes from hydroelectric plants built on its many rivers.

Servicing Needs

Surprisingly for a land rich in natural resources, half of Colombians work in the service industries. These include the government, banks, hospitals, schools, and tourism. The coastal town of Cartagena is the most popular tourist destination for foreign visitors. Wealthy Colombians take vacations on the Caribbean islands.

Brighter Future

Colombia's future is positive. Some rebel groups are agreeing to peace talks, and the drug cartels are being defeated. However, in the process, rural Colombians are still being forced from their villages. It is uncertain whether the booming economy will be enough to provide jobs for these displaced people, and ensure Colombia remains a leading nation in South America.

▲ Women and children pan for gold at a mine in the Chocó region. Mining is dirty work—and can be dangerous.

Add a Little Extra to Your Country Report!

I f you are assigned to write a report about Colombia, you'll want to include basic information about the country, of course. The Fast Facts chart on page 8 will give you a good start. The rest of the book will provide the details you need to create a full and up-to-date paper or PowerPoint presentation. But what can you do to make your report more fun than anyone else's? If you use your imagination and dig a bit deeper into some of the topics introduced in this book, you're sure to come up with information that will make your report unique!

>Flag

Perhaps you could explain the history of Colombia's flag, and the meanings of its colors. Go to **www.crwflags.com/fotw/flags** for more information.

>National Anthem

How about downloading Colombia's national anthem, and playing it for your class? At **www.nationalanthems.info** you'll find what you need, including the words to the anthem, plus sheet music for it. Simply pick "C" and then "Colombia" from the list on the left-hand side of the screen, and you're on your way.

>Time Difference

If you want to understand the time difference between Colombia and where you are, this Web site can help: **www.worldtimeserver.com**. Just pick "Colombia" from the list on the left. If you called someone in Colombia right now, would you wake them up from their sleep?

>Currency

Another Web site will convert your money into pesos, the currency used in Colombia. You'll want to know how much money to bring if you're ever lucky enough to travel to Colombia: **www.xe.com/ucc**.

>Weather

Why not check the current weather in Colombia? It's easy—go to **www.weather.com** to find out if it's sunny or cloudy, warm or cold in Colombia right now! Pick "World" from the headings at the top of the page. Then search for Colombia. Click on any city. Be sure to click on the tabs below the weather report for Sunrise/Sunset information, Weather Watch, and Business Travel Outlook, too. Scroll down the page for the 36-hour Forecast and a satellite weather map. Compare your weather to the weather in the Colombian city you chose. Is this a good season, weather-wise, for a person to travel to Colombia?

>Miscellaneous

Still want more information? Simply go to National Geographic's World Atlas for Young Explorers at **http://www.nationalgeographic.com/kids-world.atlas/**. It will help you find maps, photos, music, games, and other features that you can use to jazz up your report.

Glossary

Annual occurring every year.

Archaeologist a person who studies the remains of ancient people to learn more about how people lived in the past.

Cartel a group of several organizations that works together. Colombia's drug-producing gangs often work as cartels.

Cassava the root of a shrub that is used for food. Cassava is originally from South America but is now grown in Africa and Asia. Cassava can be fried, boiled, and mashed like potatoes or made into flour for dumplings.

Civilization when a society develops a well-organized way of life.

Climate the average weather of a certain place at different times of year.

Colony a region that is ruled by a nation located somewhere else in the world. Settlers from that distant country take the land from the region's original inhabitants.

Culture a collection of beliefs, traditions, and styles that belongs to people living in a certain part of the world.

Democracy a country that is ruled by a government chosen by all its people through elections.

Dictator a leader who has complete control over a country and does not have to be elected or re-elected to office regularly. Dictators are often cruel and corrupt.

Economy the system by which a country creates wealth through making and trading in products.

Empire territories located in several parts of the world that are controlled by a single nation.

Ethnic group a section of a country's population with members that share a common ancestry or background.

Exported transported and sold outside the country of origin.

Fertile capable of supporting new life.

Habitat a part of the environment that is suitable for certain plants and animals.

Illegal against the law.

Imported brought into the country from abroad.

Isthmus a narrow strip of land surrounded by the sea, which connects two larger regions.

Lahar a mudslide created by a volcanic eruption.

Natural resources naturally occurring materials and substances that can be collected and sold. Natural resources include oil, metals, or lumber.

Peninsula a narrow piece of land that is surrounded by water on three sides. The word means "almost island" in Latin.

Primate a type of animal that includes monkeys, apes, and lemurs.

Republic a country that is ruled by an elected head of state, such as a president.

Species a type of organism; animals or plants in the same species look similar and can only breed successfully among themselves.

Tributary a small river that flows into a larger one, adding to the amount of water in the system. The area drained by a river, including its tributaries, is called a basin.

Bibliography

Boraas, Tracey. *Colombia.* Mankato, MN: Bridgestone Books, 2002.

DuBois, Jill. *Colombia.* New York, NY: Marshall Cavendish, 2002.

Lim, Bee Hong. *Welcome to Colombia.* Milwaukee, WI: Gareth Stevens Publishing, 2000.

http://news.bbc.co.uk/1/hi/world/americas/country_profiles/1212798.stm (general information)

http://www.state.gov/r/pa/ei/bgn/35754.htm (background information from the U.S. State Department)

Further Information

NATIONAL GEOGRAPHIC Articles

Griswold, Eliza. "Medellin: Stories from an Urban War." NATIONAL GEOGRAPHIC (MARCH 2005): 72-91.

Web sites to explore

More fast facts about Colombia, from the CIA (Central Intelligence Agency): https://www.cia.gov/library/publications/the-world-fact-book/geos/co.html

Take a closer look at the geography of Colombia by downloading the detailed maps from the country's official tourism web site. The site also contains some great images from around the country: http://www.turismocolombia.com/NewsDetail.asp?ID=4722&IDCompany=127

Colombia is a vibrant and colorful place, with some amazing scenery and historic buildings. Choose a city and take a look at the images at: http://www.lonelyplanet.com/worldguide/colombia/cartagena?v=images&a=3 gallery

Juan Valdéz is one of the most famous Colombians but he doesn't even exist! Find out more about this comedy coffee grower at: http://www.juanvaldez.com/menu/Juan_Valdez/index.html

See, hear

There are many ways to get a taste of life in Colombia, such as movies, music, magazines, or TV shows. You might be able to locate these:

The Kite Festival (2004) A colorful storybook by Leyla Torres, a writer from New York, who grew up in Colombia. The Kite Festival tells the story of Fernando Flórez and his family who decide to take part in a traditional kite-flying display but have no kite to use. http://www.leylatorres.com/books.html

Gabriel García Márquez The most famous Colombian writer has written many popular books, including *One Hundred Years of Solitude* and *Love in the Time of Cholera.* Find out more about all his work at: http://www.harpercollins.com/authors/3459/Gabriel_Garcia_Marquez/index.aspx?WT.mc_id=WIKI_AUTH_GABR_041207

Bogotá Daily Find out what is happening in Colombia today by reading this English-language newspaper: http://www.bogotadaily.com

Index

Credits

Picture Credits

Front Cover – Spine: Roman Sigaev/Shutterstock; Top: Meredith Davenport/NGIC; Low Far Left: Luis Marden/NGIC; Low Left: O. Louis Mazzatenta/NGIC; Low Right: Martin Gray/NGIC; Low Far Right: Luis Marden/NGIC.

Interior – Corbis: Eliana Aponte/Reuters: 45 up; Omar Bechara Baruque/Eye Ubiquitous: 5 up; Fernando Benguecvhea/ Beateworks: 36 lo, 44 up; Richard Bickel: 2 left, 6-7, 38 up; Fredy Bulles/Reuters: 43 up; Epa: 12 lo; Owen Franken: 42 up; Gordon Gahan: TP; Lowell Georgia: 50 lo; Diego Goldberg/ Sygma: 55 up; Jeremy Horner: 3 left, 12 up, 14 lo, 15 lo, 34-35, 40 up, 41 right, 47 up, 57 up; Phillipe Lissac/Godong: 38 lo; Diego Albeiro Lopera/Reuters: 53 lo; Miguel Mendez V./epa: 56 up; Eduardo Munoz/Reuters: 11 lo; Diego Lezama Orezzoli: 14 up; Reuters: 3 right, 18 lo, 39 center, 42 lo, 45 lo, 48-49, 52 up; Stefano Rollandini/Reuters: 47 lo; Kevin Schafer: 13 center; Kevin Schafer/zefa: 2 right, 16-17; Adam Woolfitt: 26 up, 28 lo; NGIC: Sam Abell: 33 lo; Skip Brown: 21 lo; Stephen Ferry: 29 lo; Luis Marden: 20 up; O. Louis Mazzatenta: 2-3, 11 up, 24-46, 29 up, 30 lo, 31 up; Darlyne A. Murawski: 23 lo; Steve Raymer: 10 lo; Joel Sartore 22 lo, 23 up, 55 lo; Stephen St. John: 32 lo; Roy Toft: 21 up; Photos.com: 59 up; Shutterstock: Elen: 31 lo

Text copyright © 2008 National Geographic Society
Published by the National Geographic Society.
All rights reserved. Reproduction of the whole or any part of the contents without written permission from the National Geographic Society is strictly prohibited.

For information about special discounts for bulk purchases, contact National Geographic Special Sales: ngspecsales@ngs.org

For more information, please call 1-800-NGS-LINE (647-5463) or write to the following address:

NATIONAL GEOGRAPHIC SOCIETY
1145 17th Street N.W.
Washington, D.C. 20036-4688 U.S.A.

Visit the Society's Web site at www.nationalgeographic.com

Library of Congress Cataloging-in-Publication Data available on request
ISBN: 978-1-4263-0257-2

Printed in the United States of America

Series design by Jim Hiscott.
The body text is set in Avenir; Knockout.
The display text is set in Matrix Script.

Front Cover—Top: An outdoor market in Medellin; Low Far Left: Orchids in Medellin; Low Left: Cartagena; Low Right: Stone carving with jaguar teeth, San Augustín; Low Far Right: Téquendama Falls on the Bogotá River

Page 1—Children playing in Colombia. Icon image on spine, Contents page, and throughout: coffee beans

Produced through the worldwide resources of the National Geographic Society

John M. Fahey, Jr., *President and Chief Executive Officer*; Gilbert M. Grosvenor, *Chairman of the Board*; Tim T. Kelly, *President of Global Media Group*; Nina D. Hoffman, *Executive Vice President, President of Book Publishing Group*

National Geographic Staff for this Book

Nancy Laties Feresten, *Vice President, Editor-in-Chief of Children's Books*
Bea Jackson, *Director of Design and Illustration*
Jim Hiscott, *Art Director*
Virginia Koeth, *Project Editor*
Lori Epstein, *Illustrations Editor*
Stacy Gold, Nadia Hughes, *Illustrations Research Editors*
R. Gary Colbert, *Production Director*
Lewis R. Bassford, *Production Manager*
Nicole Elliott, *Manufacturing Manager*
Maps, *Mapping Specialists, Ltd.*

Brown Reference Group plc. Staff for this Book

Volume Editor: Tom Jackson
Designer: Dave Allen
Picture Manager: Clare Newman
Maps: Martin Darlison
Artwork: Darren Awuah
Index: Kay Ollerenshaw
Senior Managing Editor: Tim Cooke
Design Manager: Jeni Child
Children's Publisher: Anne O'Daly
Editorial Director: Lindsey Lowe

About the Author

DR. ANITA CROY earned her Ph.D in Spanish and Latin American studies at University College, United Kingdom. She has traveled extensively in Latin America and has written a number of books for children and young adults on various Latin American countries.

About the Consultants

ULRICH OSLENDER is a political geographer at the University of Glasgow in Scotland and has also been a visiting professor at the University of California, Los Angeles. His research focuses on the politics of social movements in Latin America, particularly in Colombia; his work is funded by the European Union Marie Curie OIF program. Since 1995 he has worked with the social movement of black communities in Colombia, and has spent over five years living and working there.

MAURICIO PARDO is a professor at the Universidad del Rosario at Bogotá, Colombia, and coordinator of the program of anthropology. He has done research on the ethnography, linguistics, history, and religion of ethnic groups and on social movements in the Pacific region in Colombia. Among his publications, he edited *Acción Colectiva y Estado en el Pacífico Colombiano* (2001), and co-edited *Panorámica Afrocolombiana Estudios Sociales del Pacífico* (2004). He is the current secretary of the Sociedad Colombiana de Antropología.

Time Line of Colombian History

B.C.

ca 15000 First people arrive from North America.

ca 3000 Farmers grow yucca and live in camps.

ca 1120 First villages are built on the Caribbean coast.

A.D.

ca 300 The Zenú people of the Caribbean coast build raised fields and canal systems to drain floodplains.

ca 800 Settlements north of modern-day Bogotá trade salt in a network that stretches 200 miles (320 km).

ca 900 The Muisca make large numbers of *tunjos*, statues of gold alloy.

1300

ca 1300 Muisca making offerings to the gods are covered in gold for the ceremony, which becomes the basis of the legend of El Dorado, "the Golden One."

ca 1350 The Tayrona perform ceremonies at the "Lost City" in the northern mountains.

1500

ca 1500 Spanish navigators explore the coast of Colombia and conquer the region, attracted by trade and stories of gold.

1510 Martín Fernández de Enciso founds Santa María, the first Spanish-speaking settlement in South America, near the present border with Panama.

1510 Vasco Balboa crosses the Isthmus of Panama and becomes the first European to see the Pacific Ocean.

1538 Spain takes control of the Muisca southern capital of Bacátá, later known as Bogotá.

1542 Colombia and Ecuador become part of the Viceroyalty of Peru, ruled from Spain.

1580 Spaniards use 8,000 laborers to try to drain Lake Guatavita to retrieve gold objects thrown into the lake as offerings to the gods.

1600

ca 1600 After fighting many native rebellions, the Spanish conquer the last Tayrona chiefs.

1700

1717 Colombia joins the Viceroyalty of New Granada, which covers much of northern South America.

1800

1810 Cartagena sets up a ruling council independent of the occupying French government, but loyal to the deposed Spanish king; it is followed by Bogotá.

1819 Revolutionary Simón Bolívar defeats the Spanish at Boyacá and founds Gran Colombia, which also includes modern-day Ecuador, Panama, and Venezuela.

1835 Colombia becomes independent after the collapse of Gran Colombia.

1899 A civil war breaks out between Liberals and Conservatives. "The War of the Thousand Days" lasts over three years, leaves 10,000 dead, and causes economic crisis.